DIY
FEARLESS FASHION

FIERCE FASHIONS,
ACCESSORIES, AND STYLES THAT POP

By Rebecca Rissman

COMPASS POINT BOOKS
a capstone imprint

Compass Point Books are published by Capstone
1710 Roe Crest Drive, North Mankato, Minnesota 56003
www.capstonepub.com

Library of Congress Cataloging-in-Publication Data
Library of Congress Cataloging-in-Publication data is available on the
Library of Congress website.
ISBN 978-1-5435-1100-0 (library binding)
ISBN 978-0-7565-6098-0 (eBook PDF)

Editorial Credits
Mandy Robbins, editor; Heather Kindseth and Heidi Thompson, designers;
Tracy Cummins, media researcher; Marcy Morin and Sarah Schuette,
photo stylists; Kathy McColley, production specialist

Photo Credits
Images by Capstone Studio: Karon Dubke
Craft Project Producer: Jodi Roelofs
Design Elements by Shutterstock

Printed and bound in the USA

PA017

TABLE OF CONTENTS

BE FEARLESS WITH YOUR FASHIONS

Are you sick of feeling like you're dressed like everyone else? Does your local department store seem dull? If you're ready to step out of those cookie cutter styles and into something fresh and fierce, then this book is for you!

Here's some more good news! Looking edgy and chic doesn't have to cost much. Just dig around in your closet for some stale styles. Then make a quick trip to your local hardware and craft stores. Your next statement ensemble is only hours and a few dollars away.

Making your own accessories and clothing is a great way to express yourself. Use the tutorials in this book to create fashions that are uniquely you.

BEFORE YOU START CREATING, GATHER SOME SUPPLIES:

beads

black permanent marker

bleach and bleach pen

cotton twine

crimp ends

crimp tubes

duct tape

fabric glue

fabric paint markers

fabric zippers

garbage bags

hardware, such as nuts or washers

hot glue gun and glue

jewelry wire

lobster clasps and jump rings

metal jewelry chains

needle nose pliers

pencil

round nose pliers

scissors

several old T-shirts

white chalk

wire cutters

zippers

JEWELRY LINGO

-Lobster clasps and jump rings are used to close necklaces and bracelets.

-Crimp ends are small metal clamps you can place at the end of a fabric, ribbon, or leather necklace or bracelet.

-Crimp tubes are tiny tubes you can use to close a wire loop.

-Beading wire is very thin wire you can string beads onto.

FREAKY FRINGE

Fierce fashionista rule number one: Don't throw away fabric scraps! They may come in handy for your next great look. Gather your T-shirt scraps for this craft. You can turn a plain chain into a perfect accessory.

WHAT YOU NEED:

T-shirt scraps
scissors
rose gold chain necklace
4 clothespins
clothes hanger
rubber gloves
dark fabric dye
water
large, wide bowl

STEPS:

1. Cut your T-shirt scraps into 20 thin strips. They should be at least 10 inches (25.5 centimeters) long. Try to make them about 0.3 inch (0.8 cm) wide. They don't need to be exact. Pull gently on the ends of each strip to stretch it into a rope.

2. Lay your chain on a flat surface. Fold one T-shirt strip in half and slip the folded end underneath the chain.

3. Pull the two loose ends over the chain and through the loop. Use one hand to hold the chain still and pull the knot tightly with the other hand.

4. Add more T-shirt string knots to either side to build up your necklace. Add strips until the necklace is as wide as you want. Use your scissors to trim the ends to form a gentle arc.

5. Use the clothespins to clip the knots of your necklace to the clothes hanger so that the chain of the necklace is straight and the fringe hangs down.

6. Put on the rubber gloves, and mix the fabric dye with water in the large bowl. Follow the directions on the package.

7. Hold the top of the hanger and carefully dip the bottom third of the fringe into the dye. Hold it so that the fringe can soak up the fabric dye for the amount of time stated in the directions.

8. Carefully lift the necklace out of the dye. Immediately rinse it under hot water until the water runs clear. Lay it flat to dry.

STYLE TIP:
EXPERIMENT WITH DIFFERENT SHAPES. TRY CUTTING THE STRIPS ON AN ANGLE TO MAKE A TRIANGLE-SHAPED NECKLINE.

BRAIDED FRINGE NECKLACE

This T-shirt necklace takes an unexpected turn with a chunky braid and extra-long fringe. Use bold colors for a wow-worthy accessory. You'll need longer strips of T-shirts for this craft, so get an extra-large T-shirt.

WHAT YOU NEED:

XL T-shirt that makes 3- to 6- foot (0.9- to 1.8- meter) long strings
scissors
leather cord
rubber band
masking tape
3 to 5 metal charms

STEPS:

1. Lay your T-shirt on a flat surface. Cut along the bottom edge to remove the hem.

2. Cut 0.5-inch (1.3-cm) strips of fabric across the width of the shirt to create large loops. Do this until you have 12 to 21 strips. The more strips you use, the wider your necklace will be.

3. Gently stretch each loop until it forms a rope-like cord.

4. Cut each loop to form a long strip. Set one strip aside. You will use it to tie your braids at the end.

5. Cut a strip of leather cord that is the same length as the T-shirt strips.

6. Gather your strips together, including the leather cord, and secure one end with the rubber band. Leave a tail of about 8 inches (20 cm). Tape the end to a flat surface.

7. Divide the strips into three groups, and braid them to form a long cord. Stop when you've reached your desired necklace length. Make sure to leave about 8 inches (20 cm) of T-shirt strands at the bottom of your braid.

8. Remove the rubber band and tape from the end of the braid.

9. Bring both ends of the braid together. Use the last strand to tie them together tightly. Secure with a double knot.

10. Trim any excess off the loose ends to have a fringe about 8 inches (20 cm) long.

11. Finally, attach your charms to a few pieces of the fringe. Vary the height so that they don't all fall at the same spot.

T-SHIRTS AND HARDWARE

Combine soft T-shirt strings and hard, shiny metal for a fierce accessory. The directions below create a necklace, but you could make a bracelet this way too.

WHAT YOU NEED:

T-shirt scraps
scissors
ruler
masking tape
10 large washers
needle nose pliers
1-inch (2.5-cm) gold crimp ends
lobster claw clasp and
jump ring

STEPS:

1. Cut the T-shirt scraps into three strips that are about 1 inch (2.5 cm) wide and 20 to 24 inches (50 to 60 cm) long. Gently pull on each end of the strips to stretch them into long ropes.

2. Gather the ends of the strings together and tape them to a desk or table.

3. Braid the three strands together to form a 5-inch (13-cm) braid.

4. Thread two washers onto the unbraided end of the three strands. Slide them all the way down until they meet the braid.

5. Pull the three strands up and over the second washer. Then thread them through the first washer. Pull tightly.

6. Now pull the three strands back through the second washer. Pull tightly.

7. Repeat these steps to string on the remaining washers.

8. After you've added your last washer, braid the remaining length of the strands.

9. Try on the necklace. Trim it to your desired length with the scissors.

10. Use the needle nose pliers to clamp the crimp ends onto each end of the necklace.

11. Use the pliers to attach the lobster clasp and jump ring to each crimp end.

VELVET AND CHAINS CHOKER

Chokers were the hottest accessory during the 1990s. Now they're back and better than ever. Try this look that mixes sweet, soft velvet with chunky metal chains.

WHAT YOU NEED:

measuring tape
wire cutters
thin jewelry chain
thicker jewelry chain
12 inches (30.5 cm) of ribbon about 1-inch (2.5-cm) thick
scissors
fabric glue
tweezers
hot glue
needle nose pliers
1-inch (2.5-cm) crimp ends
1 lobster claw

STEPS:

1. Measure around the narrowest part of your neck. Use your wire cutters to cut lengths of chain to this measurement.

2. Add about 0.5 inch (1.3 cm) to that measurement for your choker. Cut your ribbon to match that measurement.

3. Lay the ribbon out flat, with the velvet side up. Use the fabric glue to draw a straight line where you want to glue the thin chain. Leave a little space on either edge for the crimp end to clamp shut.

4. Immediately place the thin chain on top of the glue. Use a pair of tweezers to straighten the chain so that it lays flat.

5. Glue the thick chain to the ribbon just as you did the thin one. Let it dry for an hour.

5

6. Place the crimp ends on either side of the exposed ribbon. Put a dab of hot glue on each end. Use the pliers to pinch the crimp ends down over the glue.

7. Use your wire cutters to cut a 2-inch (5-cm) length of the thin jewelry chain.

8. Attach the lobster hook to one of the crimp ends.

9. Attach the thin chain to the other crimp end.

STYLE TIP:
GET WILD! CUSTOMIZE YOUR CHOKER WITH RHINESTONES, STUDS, OR EVEN SPIKES.

HEXAGONAL NUT BRACELET

Sometimes the best fashion supplies can be found in unusual places. Your local hardware store should have exactly what you need for your next edgy look.

WHAT YOU NEED:

three 36-inch (91-cm) strands of leather cord

masking tape

20 small hexagonal nuts

scissors

STEPS:

1. Tie the three strands of cord in a knot. Leave a 2-inch (5-cm) tail. Tape the tail end of the cord to a flat surface.

2. Begin braiding the three strands together. Keep the string taught. Make your braid nice and tight.

3. When you've braided about 4 inches (10 cm), slide a hexagonal nut onto the strand on the right. Slide it all the way up until it bumps into the braid. Then cross it over the center strand. Use your thumb to hold the nut in place.

4. Slide a hexagonal nut onto the strand on the left. Slide it all the way up until it bumps into the braid. Then cross it over the center strand. Use your thumb to hold the nut in place.

5. Continue adding nuts as you braid. Be careful to keep the cord taut, and hold each nut in place as you braid it.

6. After you've threaded all the nuts into the braid, continue braiding the cord for another 4 inches (10 cm) or so. Cut it so that it wraps around your wrist twice. Tie a knot at the base of the braid.

SKELETON BRACELET

The stacked hardware on this bracelet resembles an animal's backbone. Use small wing nuts to create an everyday accessory. You could also use an oversized version for a bolder statement piece.

1. Cut a length of craft wire that is about 1 inch (2.5 cm) longer than the length around your wrist.

2. Thread your lobster clasp onto the end of the wire. Fold the wire onto itself. Then slip the crimp tube over the wire end. The folded wire will form a loop. Use your pliers to pinch the crimp firmly into place.

3. Slide one of the two smaller hexagonal nuts onto the wire.

4. Thread a larger hexagonal nut on next followed by a wing nut.

5. Continue threading on the larger hexagonal nuts and wing nuts, making sure the wing nuts are all facing the same direction.

6. Add the other very small silver hexagonal nut at the end.

7. Thread your jump ring onto the wire and then fold the wire over itself.

8. Slip the crimp tube onto the wire to make a small loop. Use the pliers to pinch the crimp firmly into place.

STYLE TIP:
MIX UP BRASS AND SILVER HARDWARE FOR AN EYE-CATCHING LOOK.

COMIC BOOK BANGLES

Zap! Wham! Bang! Channel your inner superhero with this amazing craft. These bangles pack quite the punch. Pow!

WHAT YOU NEED:

scissors
old comic books
2 wooden or plastic bracelets of different widths
small paintbrush
craft glue

STEPS:

1. Flip through some old comic books, and cut out 10 to 15 small panels.

2. Cut out a few small word bubbles.

3. Use the paintbrush to apply craft glue to a small area outside and inside of your bangle.

4. While the glue is still wet, apply a comic strip to the outside of the bangle. Wrap the edges around the bracelet. If you have enough left over, fold it into the inner edge of the bracelet.

5. Working in sections, continue applying glue and comic book strips around the outside.

6. Glue smaller images inside the bangle to cover up any exposed wood or plastic.

7. If you have any spaces left on the front of the bangle that need to be covered, coat the area with glue. Place your small word bubbles over them.

8. While the glue is still wet, gently press down on the comic book panels. Do this all around the bracelet to flatten out any wrinkles or bumps.

9. Paint a final coat of glue all over the outside and inside of the bracelet. Let the bracelet dry overnight.

STYLE TIP:
IF YOUR BANGLES ARE CURVED, YOUR COMIC BOOK STRIPS WON'T LAY PERFECTLY FLAT ACROSS THEM. DON'T WORRY! JUST MAKE SMALL FOLDS IN THE PAPER TO HELP IT CONTOUR TO THE SIDES OF THE BANGLE.

ZIP IT

Zippers aren't just for closing your bag or keeping your jeans on. They can be the perfect building blocks for edgy accessories. Look for zippers with chunky metallic teeth.

STEPS:

1. Unzip the two zippers. Line three of the four zipper strips next to each other on a table.

2. Stack the three strips on top of one another and carefully add a very small line of hot glue along the top edge of the stack.

3. Quickly, while the glue is still hot, slide a crimp end over the glued end. Use the needle nose pliers to clamp it down firmly.

4

ZIPPER ART:
Twist, roll, and wind one half of a zipper up to make amazing shapes. Add a little hot glue to make your zipper sculpture permanent. Wear it on a necklace as a pendant, or make a couple and turn them into a pair of earrings.

4. Braid the three strips together.

5. Pinch the bottom edges together. Snip any uneven ends of the fabric to make them match up.

6. Apply a thin line of hot glue along the edge of the stack of zipper strips. Quickly clamp the other leather crimp on the end.

7. Use the needle nose pliers to attach the lobster clasp to one side and the jump ring to the other side.

STYLE TIP:
BE VERY CAREFUL WITH THE HOT GLUE GUN. HOT GLUE CAN BURN YOUR SKIN!

MIDI CHAIN RINGS

Midi rings sit in the middle of your finger. Try out this unexpected design to learn the basics of ring making. You can then push your creativity with more designs of your own.

WHAT YOU NEED:

20-gauge black jewelry wire

ruler

wire cutters

gold chain

gold beads

round nose pliers

cylindrical object that is similar to the width of your finger, such as a marker

STEPS:

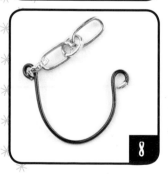

CHAIN LENGTH RING

1. Cut a length of wire 1.5 inch (3.75 cm) long.

2. Cut a length of gold chain 0.5 inch (1.5 cm) long.

3. Wrap the wire all the way around the tip of your pliers to make a tiny loop.

4. Slide the long end of the wire through an end ring of the chain. Then pull the chain all the way down the wire until it is inside the loop. Use the pliers to pinch the wire loop closed, keeping the chain inside.

5. Now shape your ring. Press the length of your wire around your cylindrical object until it is shaped like a C.

6. Try the ring on for size. It should sit between your top two knuckles.

7. Use the wire cutters to trim any extra wire, making sure to leave enough for your second loop.

8. Use the pliers to make the second loop on the wire.

9. Slide the last ring of the loose chain onto the loop. Squeeze the loop shut with your pliers.

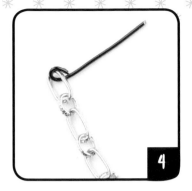

BAR AND BEAD RING

1. Cut a 1-inch (2.5-cm) length of chain.

2. Cut a 0.5-inch (1.5-cm) length of wire.

3. Slide one end of your wire through the last ring in the chain.

4. Use your pliers to make a loop and pinch it shut.

5. Drape the ring over your finger to make sure the length is okay. Use your wire cutters to trim any excess chain.

6. Slide 2 or 3 gold beads onto your piece of wire.

7. Thread the end of the wire through the last ring in the chain.

8. Use your pliers to make a tiny loop and pinch it shut.

STYLE TIP:
WEAR THESE MIDI RINGS ALONE OR STACK THEM!

FAUX SEPTUM PIERCING

Facial piercings make a bold statement. But they're also a big commitment and painful to get. For a painless look, try this faux septum piercing.

WHAT YOU NEED:

20-gauge jewelry wire
ruler
wire cutters
round nose pliers
scissors
beading wire
small silver or gold beads

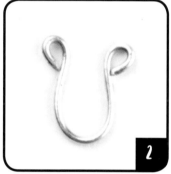

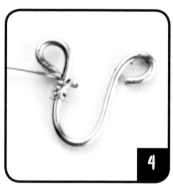

STEPS:

1. Use your wire cutters to cut 1 inch (2.5 cm) of wire. Bend the wire into a U shape.

2. Grip the end of the wire with your round nose pliers. Bend the wire outward to form a very small loop. Repeat on the other side.

3. Use your scissors to cut a section of beading wire that is about 4 inches (10 cm) long.

4. Pinch one end of the beading wire just below one of the loops and tightly wrap it around the wire several times to secure it in place.

5. Use your scissors to snip off any tail end of the beading wire. Wrap the wire over the cut end another few times to make sure the sharp wire is covered.

6. Slide one bead all the way down the beading wire until it rests against the septum ring. Holding the bead in place, wrap the beading wire around the septum ring once.

7. Slide another bead on, and wrap the beading wire around again. Make sure the wire is nice and snug. You want the beads to sit right next to each other.

9

8. Continue adding beads and wrapping the wire until you get to the loop on the other side of the septum ring.

9. After the last bead, wrap the beading wire around the septum ring a few times.

10. Snip the wire as close to the ring as you can. Use your pliers to pinch the sharp end down.

EAR CUFF WITH CHAINS

Try this bold ear cuff for a change of pace. The half-heart shape helps it sit comfortably behind your ear. The dangling chains add a surprising touch of drama.

WHAT YOU NEED:

wire cutter
ruler
18-gauge jewelry wire
round nose pliers
jewelry chain

STEPS:

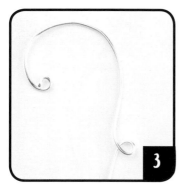

1. Cut a 6-inch (15-cm) length of wire. Use the round nose pliers to form a loop at one end of the wire. This will be the part of the ear cuff that shows at the top of your ear.

2. Use your hands to curve the wire into a half-heart shape, checking often to see how it fits on your ear.

3. About halfway down the heart, clamp the wire with your pliers, and wrap the bottom end of the wire out, over, and down. This forms a loop projecting out away from the center of the half heart.

4. Use your wire cutters to cut a 3-inch (7.5-cm) length of chain. Thread the end of the chain onto the bottom of the heart and slide it all the way up until it is inside the loop you just made.

5. Use your pliers to squeeze the loop together to secure the chain in place.

6. Repeat steps 3 through 5 three more times as you move down the length of the heart.

7. When you finish looping your chain onto the last ring, snip off any excess wire. Use your pliers to close the loop and tuck any sharp wire.

8. Try on the cuff one more time to be sure it fits your ear. Make any adjustments necessary to make it feel comfortable and secure.

STYLE TIP:
CUSTOMIZE THIS LOOK. ADD BEADS TO THE END OF YOUR CHAINS, OR ADD A LONG CHAIN TO THE LOOP AT THE TOP OF YOUR EAR.

EDGY
FLOWER CROWN

Flower crowns are usually pretty and sweet. Try this version with black flowers, silver chains, and rhinestones for a dark twist.

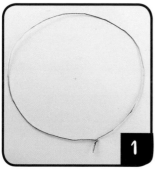

STEPS:

1. Wrap the wire around your head to see how big your crown will be. Add about 1 inch (2.5 cm), and snip the wire. Twist the ends of the wire together to form a ring.

2. Cover the twisted wire in floral tape.

3. Use your wire cutters to cut a 10-inch (25.5-cm) string of jewelry chain.

4. Carefully hot glue one end of the chain to your crown.

5. After the glue has cooled, wrap the area with floral tape to further secure the chain in place.

6. Glue the other end of the chain to the crown about 4 inches (10 cm) away. It should hang in a nice loop.

7. When the glue has cooled, cover the area with floral tape.

8. Repeat steps 3 through 7 up to six more times around the back of your crown. Cut the chain in varying lengths. Make sure to leave a gap around the front of the crown for your face.

9. Begin filling in the crown with silver leaves. Attach each to the crown with hot glue. Then add floral tape to secure it.

10. Place your fabric flowers all around the crown. Attach each first with hot glue and then wrap the ends with floral tape.

11. Glue rhinestones around your crown.

STYLE TIP:
MIX IT UP! PLAY WITH DIFFERENT TEXTURES, COLORS, AND SHAPES. YOUR CROWN CAN BE BURSTING WITH BIG, BRIGHT FLOWERS. IF YOU WANT TO MAKE A SPLASH, ADD CHAINS OF RHINESTONES INSTEAD OF THE SILVER JEWELRY CHAINS.

CROP THAT TOP

Do you have any faded old shirts in your closet that you're ready to be done with? Don't donate them just yet. Grab your scissors, and get ready for a vintage style revolution.

WHAT YOU NEED:

thin cotton graphic T-shirt
scissors
measuring tape
white chalk

STEPS:

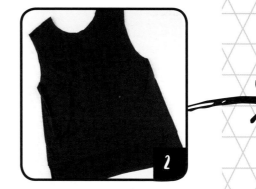

1. Lay your shirt out flat on a table with the front facing up. Cut off the collar and sleeves. Carefully cut on the inside of the seams to make sure you remove them. Try to stay as close to the lines of the seams as possible.

2. Turn the shirt over so that the back side is up. Carefully cut a horizontal line across the back of the shirt that is about 4 inches (10 cm) above the bottom hem. Be sure to keep it long enough for your school dress code if you plan to flaunt your style during class.

3. Flip the shirt over again so that the front is facing up. Cut only the bottom hem off the front of the shirt.

4. Use your measuring tape to find the middle of the front of your shirt. Make a small mark with your chalk along the bottom edge of the front of your shirt.

5. Use your chalk to draw two diagonal lines connecting the bottom center of the hem to meet the cropped edges on the back of the shirt.

6. Cut along these two diagonal lines. Make a 4-inch (10 cm) vertical cut at the center of the front of the shirt to create two triangle-shaped tails.

7. Try on the shirt to see if the fit is right. If it's too long, trim a little extra with the scissors.

SKELETON TEES

Do you want to turn an old T-shirt into something extra edgy? Add a cut-out design on the back. For an unexpected twist, try a skull or rib cage design.

STEPS:

SKULL SHIRT

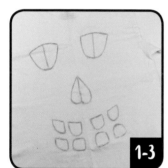

1-3

5

1. Lay your shirt on a flat surface with the back side facing up. Use the chalk to draw two large oval-shaped eyes. Draw a vertical stripe down the center of each eye.

2. Draw an upside-down heart for a nose. Draw a vertical stripe down the middle of it.

3. Add two rows of oval-shaped teeth.

4. Carefully cut out the shapes. Make sure to leave narrow strips of fabric down the center of your eyes and nose.

5. Cut the hem off of both sleeves.

6. Make a straight cut up the side of both sleeves toward the shoulder.

7. Roll the fabric of the narrow strips down the center of the eyes and nose between your fingers. This will help make these strips look extra stringy.

8. Wash the shirt according to the directions on the tag to remove the chalk.

RIB CAGE TEE

1

2

3

1. Lay the shirt on a flat surface, with the back side facing up. Lay a strip of masking tape down the center of the shirt from top to bottom.

2. Use your chalk to draw a tall, thin heart on the back of the shirt. The masking tape should be running up the center of the heart.

3. Cut horizontal slits inside each side of the heart. The slits should be about 1 to 2 inches (2.5 to 5 cm) apart.

4. Remove the masking tape. Wash the shirt according to the directions on the tag to remove the chalk.

STYLE TIP:
HOT GLUE GEMS OR STUDS DOWN THE CENTER OF THE RIB CAGE FOR A BOLDER LOOK!

DIP IT

Try out this cool color stripping technique to add an edgy touch to your dark or colored clothes. Get an adult to help you with this activity. Bleach is a dangerous chemical.

WHAT YOU NEED:

extra-long colored tank top
plastic bag
rubber band
rubber gloves
hot water
bleach
bucket
dish soap
white vinegar
scissors

STEPS:

1. Slide the top three quarters of the tank top into the plastic bag. Leave the bottom quarter hanging out. Tightly secure the bottom of the plastic bag with the rubber band. This will protect the top part of your shirt from getting splashed with bleach.

2. Go outside or to a well-ventilated area. Put on the rubber gloves. Then fill the bucket with a mixture of 2 parts hot water and 1 part bleach.

3. Carefully lower the exposed part of the tank top into the bleach mixture.

4. Let the shirt sit there until it has become light enough for your taste. You'll need to check it every 10 minutes or so. This can take anywhere from 10 to 40 minutes.

5. Wearing your rubber gloves, carefully lift the shirt out of the bleach mixture. Bring your shirt to a sink. Rinse the exposed part thoroughly. Keep the fabric inside the bag as dry as possible.

6. Wash out the bucket with soapy water. Then fill it with a mixture of 2 parts cold water, 1 part vinegar.

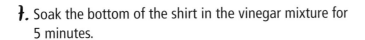

7. Soak the bottom of the shirt in the vinegar mixture for 5 minutes.

8. Remove the plastic bag and bring the shirt back to the sink for one last rinse.

9. Put the shirt into your washing machine by itself. Wash and dry it according to the directions on the tag.

10. Use your scissors to cut vertical slits every 0.5 inch (1.3 cm) around the base of the shirt. Have the slits go up to the top of the bleached section.

11. Gently pull on the strips of fabric for a ropey fringe.

12. Tie a knot at the bottom of each string to finish the look.

EMBELLISHED SHOULDER TANK

This top is as unique as you are. Choose your shoulder embellishments from a variety of colors and materials to make this piece as wow-worthy as you want.

WHAT YOU NEED:

scissors
T-shirt scraps
wire cutter
jewelry or rhinestone chain
T-shirt
needle
thread matching your
    T-shirt scraps

STEPS:

1. Cut your T-shirt scraps into long, thin ribbons. You'll want anywhere between 10-20 ribbons that are about 10 inches (25.5 cm) long.

2. Use the wire cutters to cut your jewelry or rhinestone chains into segments that are roughly the same length as the T-shirt ribbons.

3. Lay the T-shirt on a flat table.

4. Thread the needle and make a knot.

5. Use a few simple stitches to sew the center of one T-shirt ribbon onto the shoulder seam. One side of the strip should fall over the front of the shirt and the other over the back.

6

7

6. Sew the center of a length of chain next to the first T-shirt ribbon.

7. Continue adding T-shirt ribbons and chain until you've covered the shoulder seam. If you want more drama, add a second layer of ribbons and chains on top of the first. Trim any pieces that seem too long to you.

8. Cut off the sleeves of your T-shirt.

BLEACH PEN LEGGINGS

Bleach pens are handy tools for fighting stains on the go. They can also be a fabulous fashion tool. Grab an old pair of black leggings and get creative.

WHAT YOU NEED:

black leggings
paper grocery bags
rubber gloves
bleach pen

STEPS:

1. Lay your leggings out on a table or another flat work surface. Fold the paper bags into long rectangles, and slide them inside the leggings. Put on the rubber gloves.

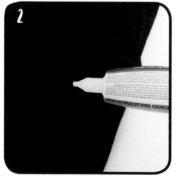

2. Use the bleach pen to draw a design around the knee on one leg. Draw more designs on the ankle and hip of the other leg.

3. Leave the bleach on the leggings until it is completely dry.

4. Remove the paper bags from inside the leggings.

5. Wearing your rubber gloves, run the leggings under water to rinse the bleach away.

6. Immediately put the leggings into a wash cycle by themselves. Wash and dry them according to the tag.

STYLE TIP:
IF DRAWING ISN'T YOUR THING, YOUR OWN HANDWRITING CAN BE ART! USE THE BLEACH PEN TO WRITE A POEM, SONG, OR PASSAGE FROM YOUR FAVORITE BOOK.

STUDDED CUFFS

Want to bring an edgy touch to your everyday clothes? Add metal studs to your cuffed jeans!

WHAT YOU NEED:

black skinny jeans
fabric pins
metal studs
needle nose pliers

STEPS:

1. Try on your jeans. Fold the ankles up twice to create cuffs.

2. Slip the jeans off, and lay them on a flat work surface.

3. Carefully use the fabric pins to secure the bottom fold of the cuff. This will keep your cuffs in place as you work.

4. Insert fabric pins along the top fold of the cuff. These are just here to remind you of how high your cuff is so that you know where to place your studs. Then unfold that top edge of the cuff.

5. Lay your studs out on the table next to the cuffed jeans to create your pattern. Get creative! Try arranging them in rows, clusters, or starbursts to see what you like the most.

6. Begin to transfer your studs to the cuffs. Push the metal prongs of each stud through the denim. You will feel the tips of the metal prongs poke out on the underside of the denim.

7. Use your pliers to fold the prongs down to secure the stud in place on the underside of the cuff.

8. Continue placing your studs on the cuff. Remember to place them all the way around, so that they show if you're facing front or back.

9. Remove the fabric pins from the top edge of the cuff and fold it back down.

10. Remove the fabric pins from the bottom fold of the cuff.

SPICE UP YOUR SHOE GAME

Soothe your shoe envy with these DIY kicks. You'll need a pair of white canvas shoes. You should be able to pick these up at your local superstore for just a few dollars.

WHAT YOU NEED:

white canvas sneakers
wet paper towel
newspapers
pencil
fabric markers

STEPS:

1. Wipe the surface of your shoes clean with the wet paper towel. Let it dry completely.

2. Stuff newspapers inside each shoe. This will make them a firm, flat surface to draw on.

3. Use the pencil to sketch swirling vines, flowers, stripes, or any other designs you like. You could even add in words or sayings that inspire you. Don't worry about making your shoes exactly the same.

4. Add your initials to the heel of each shoe. Try to come up with your own unique font. This monogram will be like a signature to your artwork.

5. Use the black fabric marker to outline your designs all over the shoe.

6. For a more dramatic look, fill in the area around your designs with black. Let the black marker dry.

7. Use colored paint markers to fill in the designs if you would like a pop of color. Let the marker dry. Then remove the newspaper stuffing.

DUCT TAPE AND TRASH BAG SKIRT

This DIY skirt is big, bold, and fabulously funky. Try it on, and strike a pose! Your friends won't believe you made it from tape and garbage bags.

WHAT YOU NEED:

- measuring tape
- roll of bright pink duct tape
- scissors
- package of 6-gallon (23 L) garbage bags
- package of 4-gallon (15 liter) garbage bags
- clear tape
- hook and loop strip

STEPS:

1. Measure your waist where you want the skirt to sit. Add 4 inches (10 cm) to that number. This will be the length of the waistband for your skirt.

2. Measure out three strips of duct tape for your waistband. Carefully lay them out with the sticky side up. Overlap the three strips by about 0.5 inch (1 cm) to stick them together and form one thick band.

3. Cut the closed bottoms off of your garbage bags. Starting with the 6-gallon bags, turn each bag on its side, so that the open ends face out to either side.

4. Stick the upper right corner of the garbage bag onto the lower right edge of the duct tape strip, about 0.5 inch (1 cm) above the bottom of the tape and about 1.5 inches (4 cm) from the end of the tape.

5. Use your fingers to form small crimps or pleats in the garbage bag. Continue sticking it to the duct tape.

6. Repeat steps 4 and 5 until you've placed crimped garbage bags along the bottom edge of the duct tape waistband, leaving about 1.5 inches (4 cm) of exposed duct tape on the other end.

7. Add another row of the crimped 6-gallon garbage bags about 1 inch (2.5 cm) up the duct tape waistband. Remember to leave your two ends of the waistband exposed.

8. Next, add a row or two of crimped garbage bags using the 4-gallon bags. This will give your skirt extra volume. Stagger the placement of your garbage bags so that there won't be any gapping when you put it on. Leave about 1 inch (2.5 cm) of exposed duct tape along the top of the waistband.

CONTINUE

DUCT TAPE AND TRASH BAG SKIRT

9. Carefully lay a strip of duct tape over the exposed section of tape along the top of your waistband. Arrange this strip of tape so that about 1 inch (2.5 cm) will overhang the top edge of the skirt. After you have laid this strip of tape down over the exposed sticky side of the waistband, flip the skirt over and fold the sticky tape down. This will ensure that no exposed sticky edges irritate your skin or stick to your shirt.

10. Flip the skirt back over, and cut strips of duct tape to cover the two tabs of exposed sticky tape on either side of your waistband. Apply these strips over the sticky tape.

11. Try the skirt on, holding one waistband tab under the other. Hold your finger down to mark the spot where they overlap, then take the skirt off again. Apply the hook and loop strip to the waistband where you want the two sides to attach.

12. Put the skirt back on. Look for any areas where the garbage bags gap. Use the clear tape to connect any garbage bags that are separating too much.

STYLE TIP: YOU CAN DRESS UP THIS LOOK FOR YOUR NEXT DANCE WITH A MORE FORMAL TOP THAT COVERS THE DUCT TAPE WAISTBAND!

OTHER BOOKS IN THIS SET

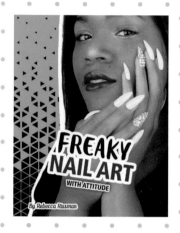

AUTHOR BIO

REBECCA RISSMAN is a nonfiction author and editor. She has written more than 300 books about history, science, and art. Her book *Shapes in Sports* earned a starred review from Booklist, and her series Animal Spikes and Spines received a 2013 Teachers' Choice Award for Children's Books from *Learning Magazine*. Rissman especially enjoys writing about fashion. She studied fashion history as part of her master's degree in English Literature at Loyola University Chicago. She lives in Chicago, Illinois, with her husband and two daughters.